SEEING STARS

The Secret Life of Starfish

DENISE ADAMS

NIMBUS
PUBLISHING LTD.
NIMBUS.CA

Nimbus Publishing Limited
3660 Strawberry Hill Street, Halifax, NS, B3K 5A9
(902) 455-4286 nimbus.ca

Printed and bound in Canada
NB1519

Library and Archives Canada Cataloguing in Publication

Title: Seeing stars : the secret life of starfish / Denise Adams.
Names: Adams, Denise, 1961- author, photographer.
Identifiers: Canadiana (print) 20200388207
Canadiana (ebook) 20200388215
ISBN 9781771089319 (softcover)
ISBN 9781771089388 (EPUB)
Classification: LCC PS8601.D443 S43 2021 | DDC jC813/.6—dc23

Canada Council for the Arts Conseil des arts du Canada

Nimbus Publishing acknowledges the financial support for its publishing activities from the Government of Canada, the Canada Council for the Arts, and from the Province of Nova Scotia. We are pleased to work in partnership with the Province of Nova Scotia to develop and promote our creative industries for the benefit of all Nova Scotians.

Disclaimer

Starfish are very sensitive and fragile creatures. The ones that appear in this book have been handled minimally and with the greatest of care. Please do not disturb starfish that you may find in the water. Should you find one beached, promptly and gently return it to sea.

For more information on how these photos were taken, please see the author's note at the back of the book.

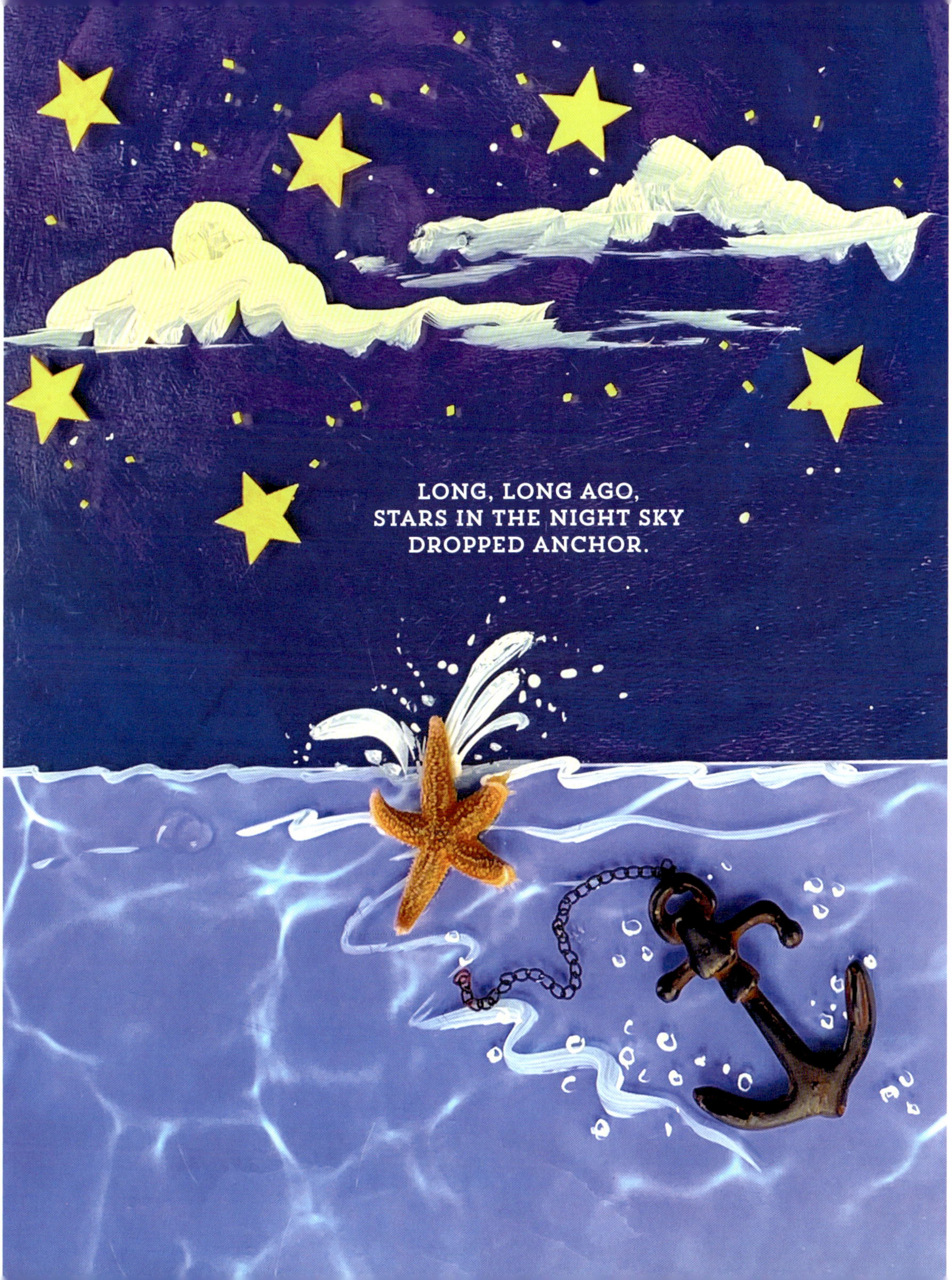

LONG, LONG AGO,
STARS IN THE NIGHT SKY
DROPPED ANCHOR.

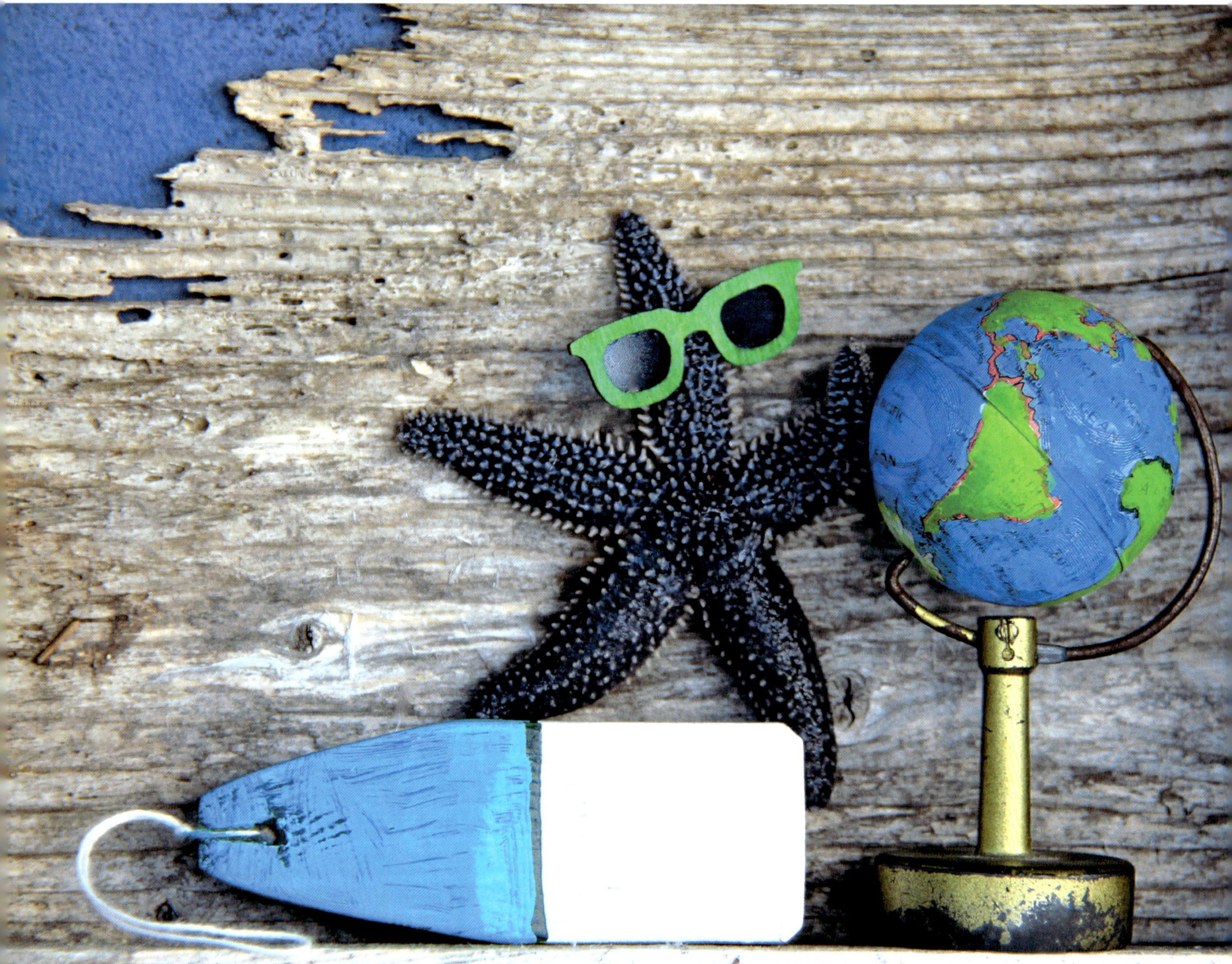

EVERY SALTY BODY OF WATER ON THE GLOBE HAS STARFISH!

AHHH! THE LIFE OF A STAR.

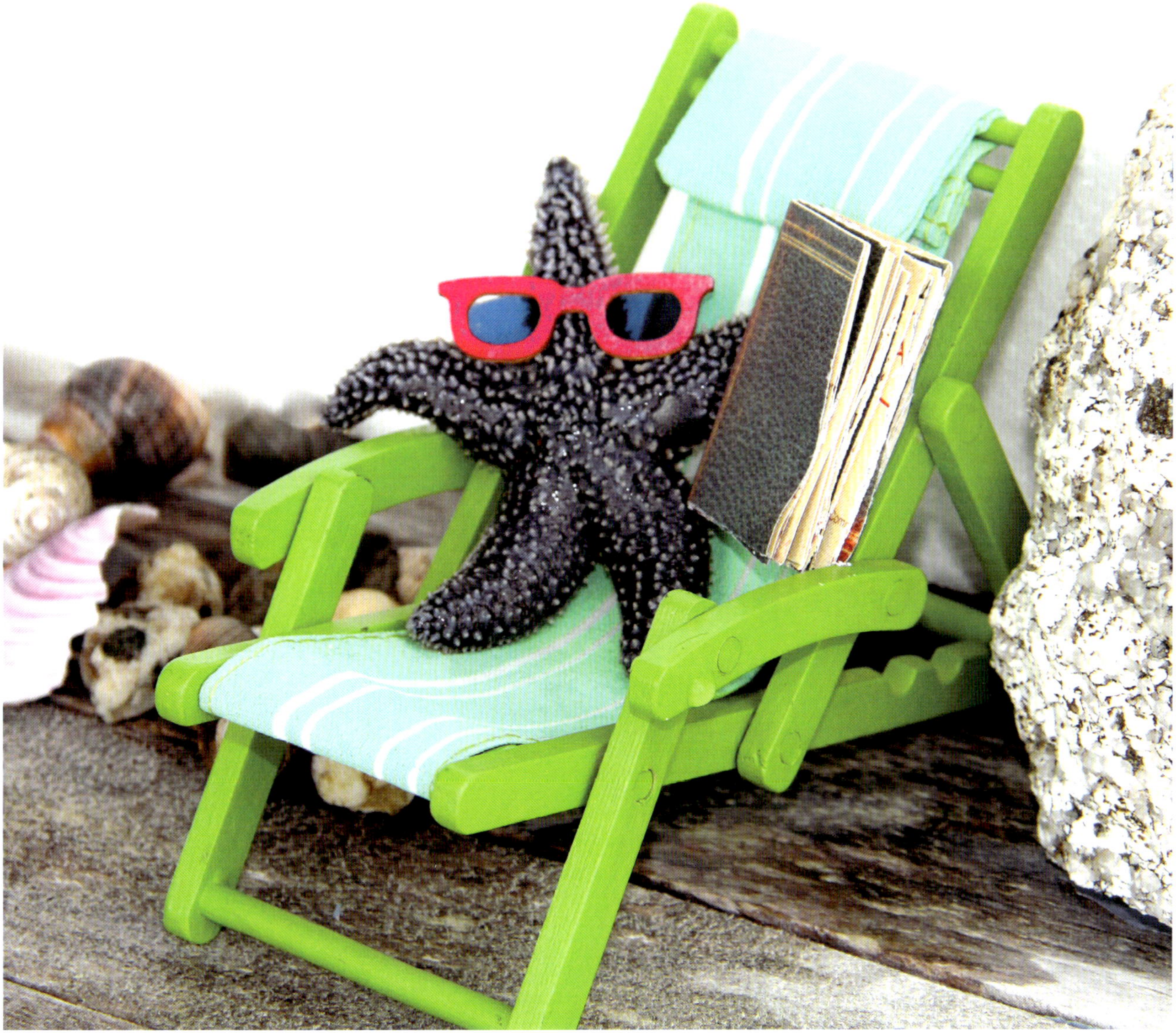

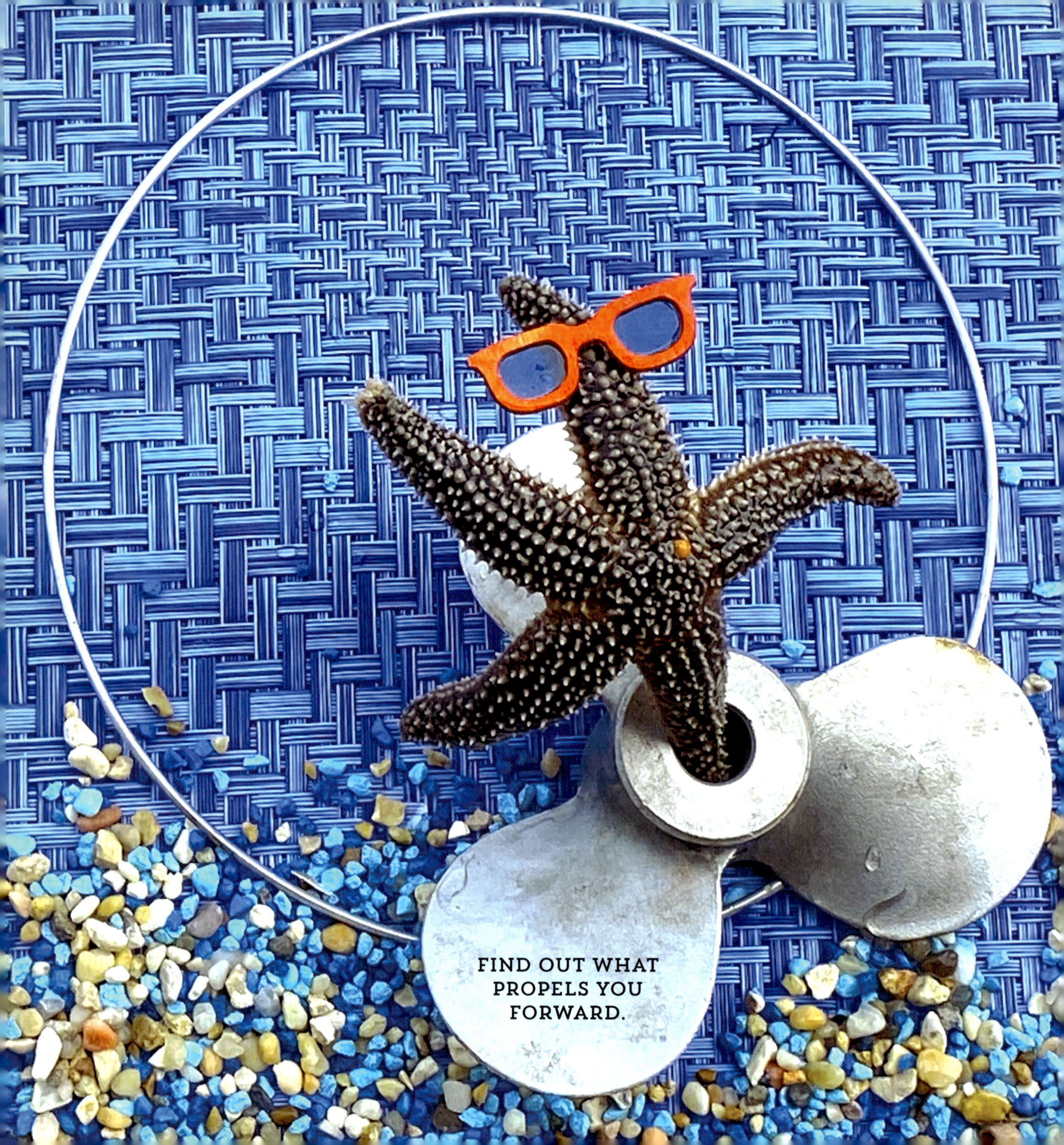
FIND OUT WHAT
PROPELS YOU
FORWARD.

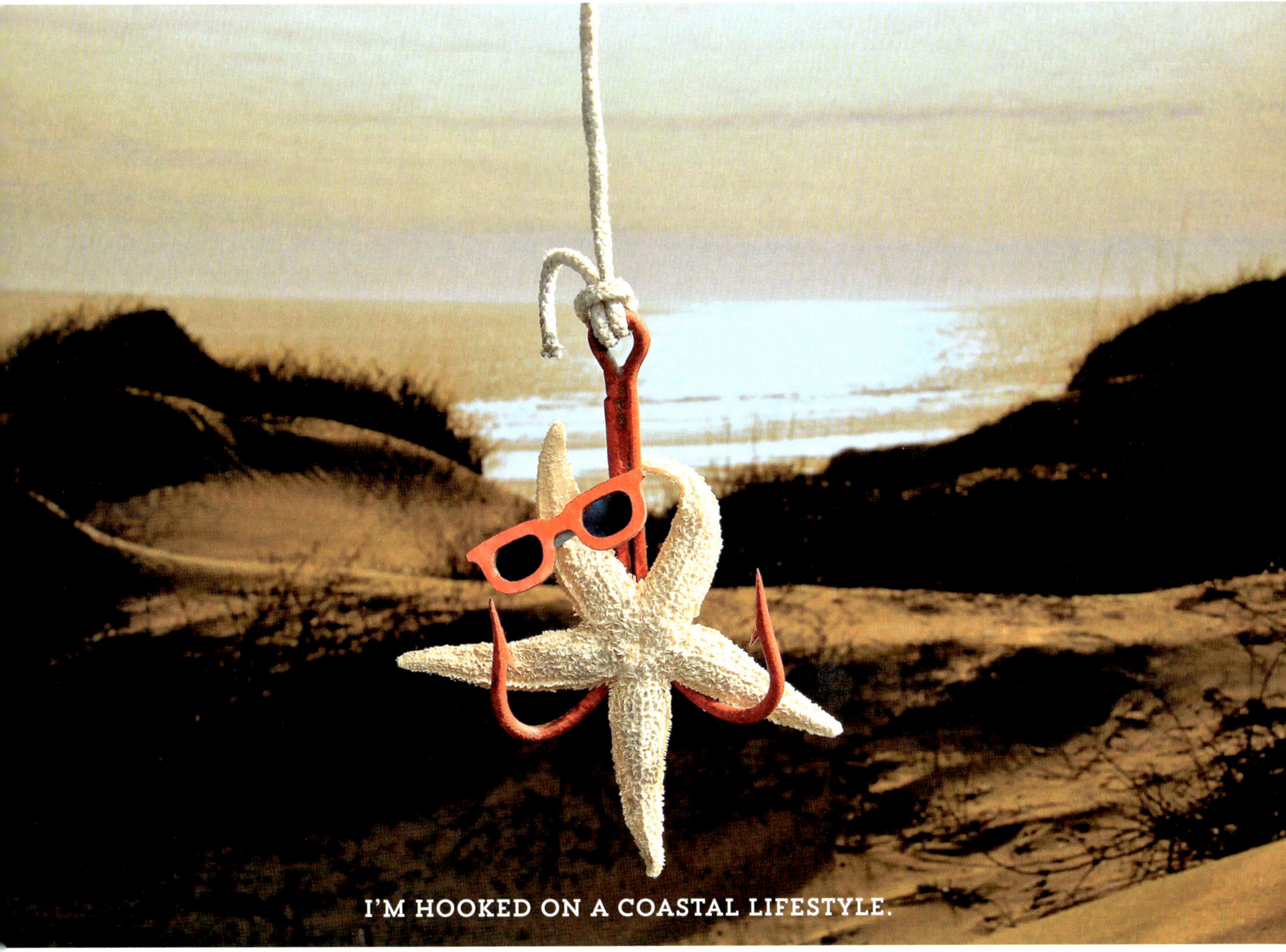
I'M HOOKED ON A COASTAL LIFESTYLE.

BET YOU DIDN'T KNOW THAT STARFISH CAN'T SWIM.

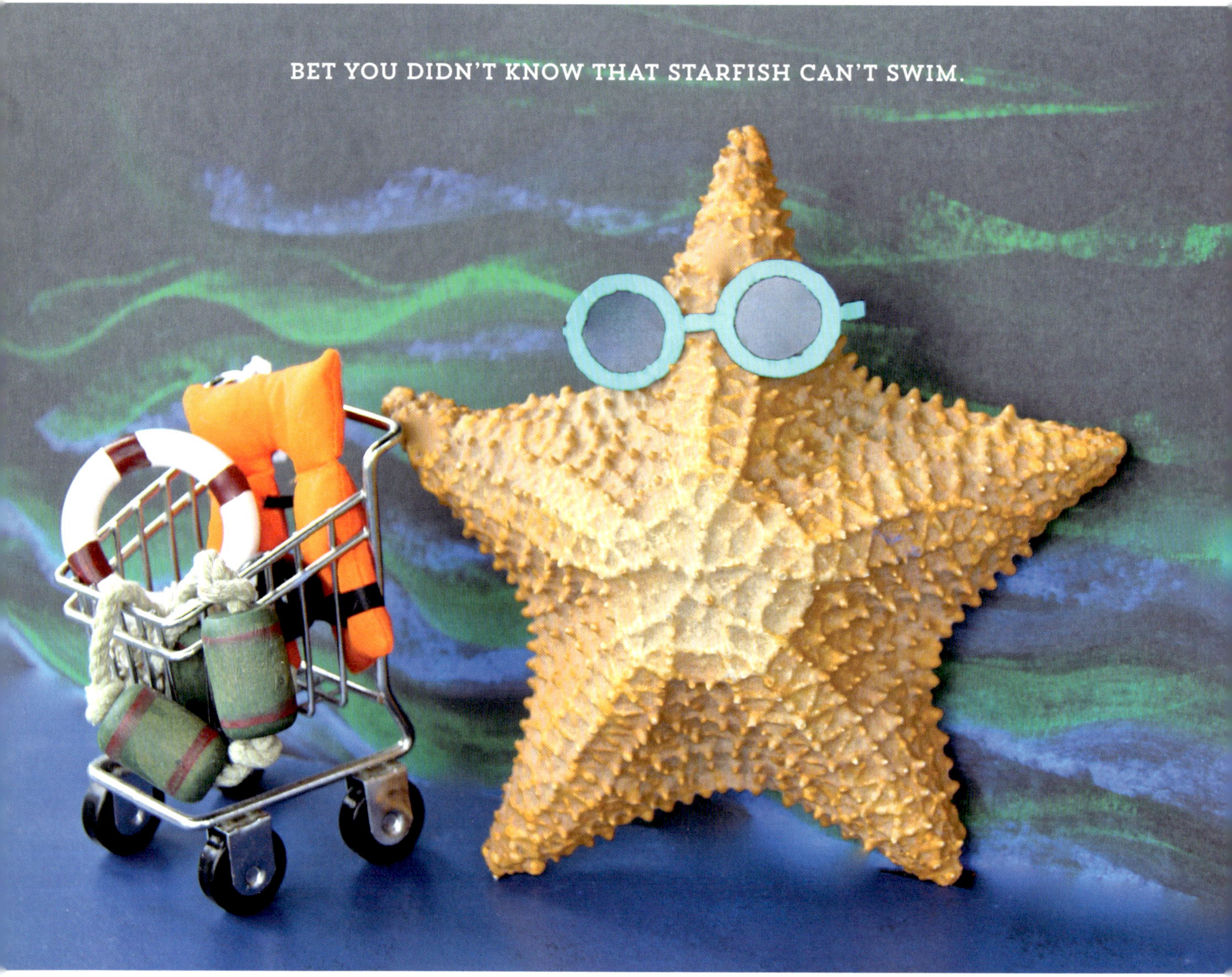

YOU COULD CALL ME A DRIFTER.

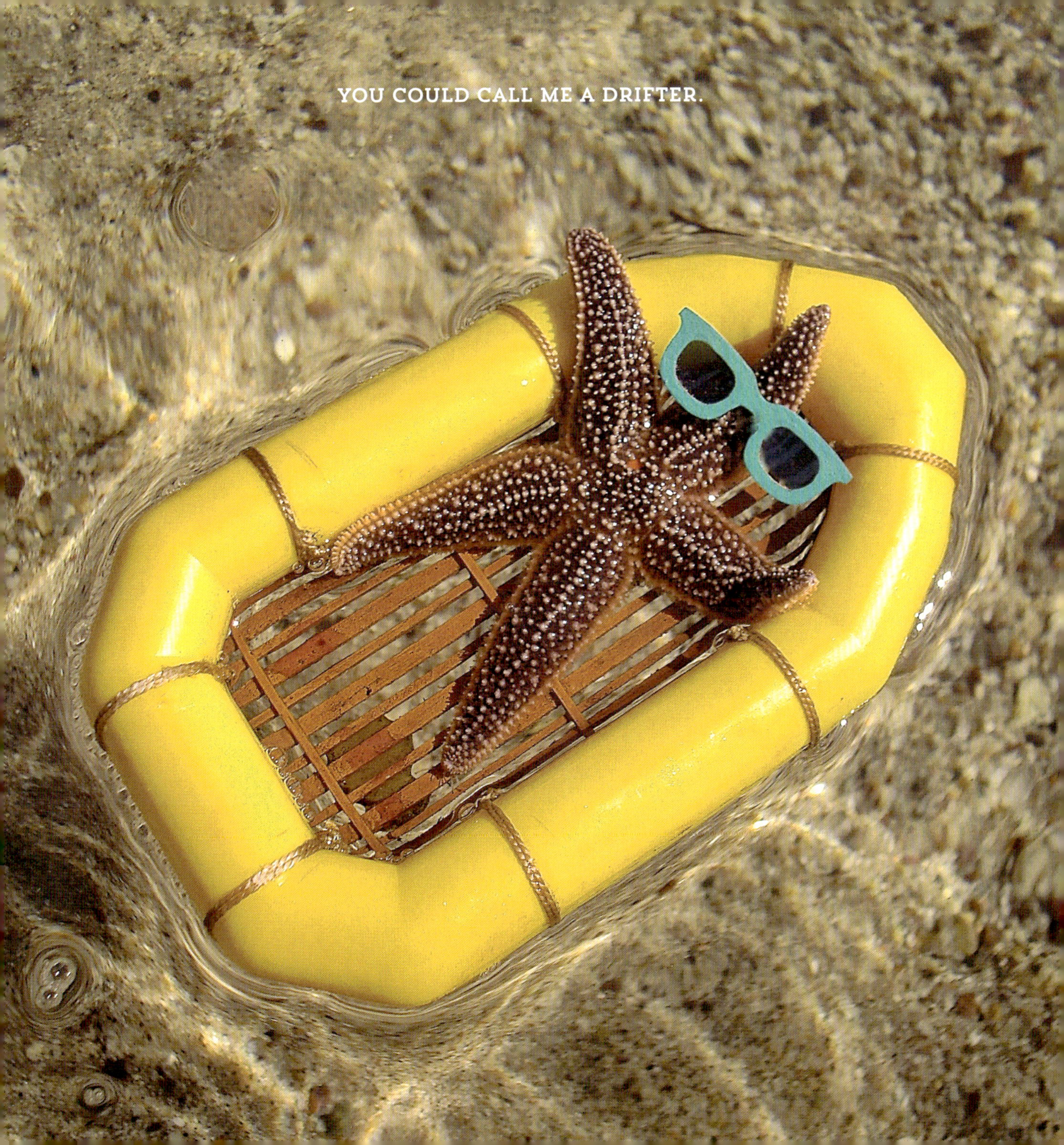

I LOVE YOU INSIDE OUT.

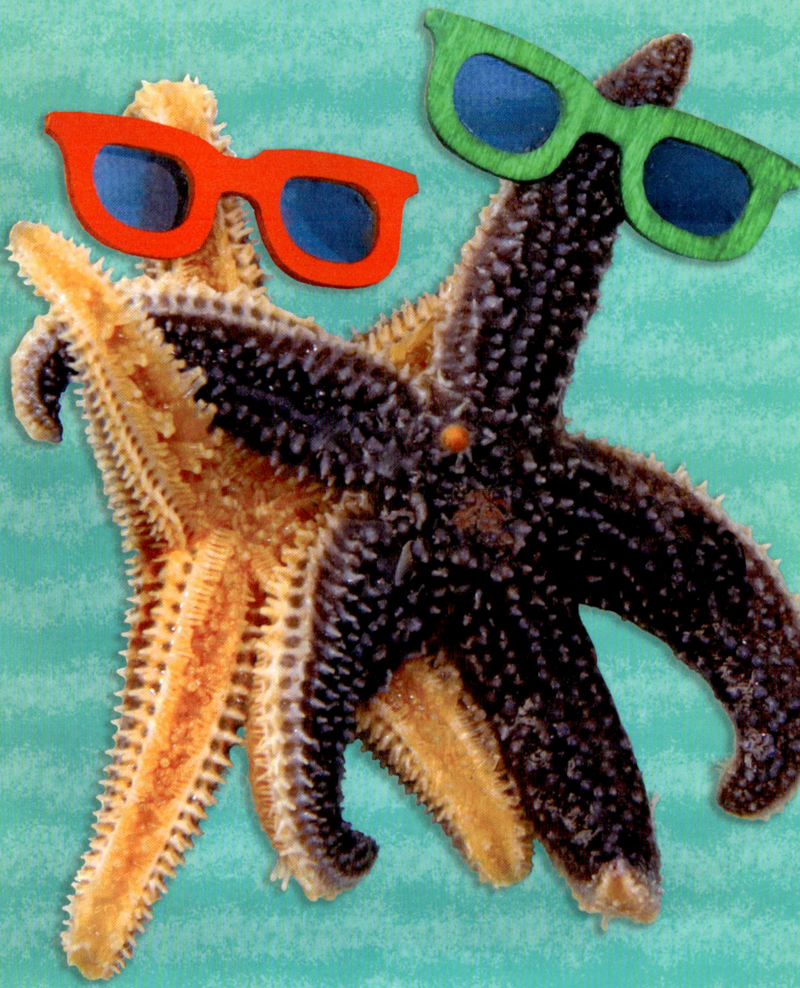

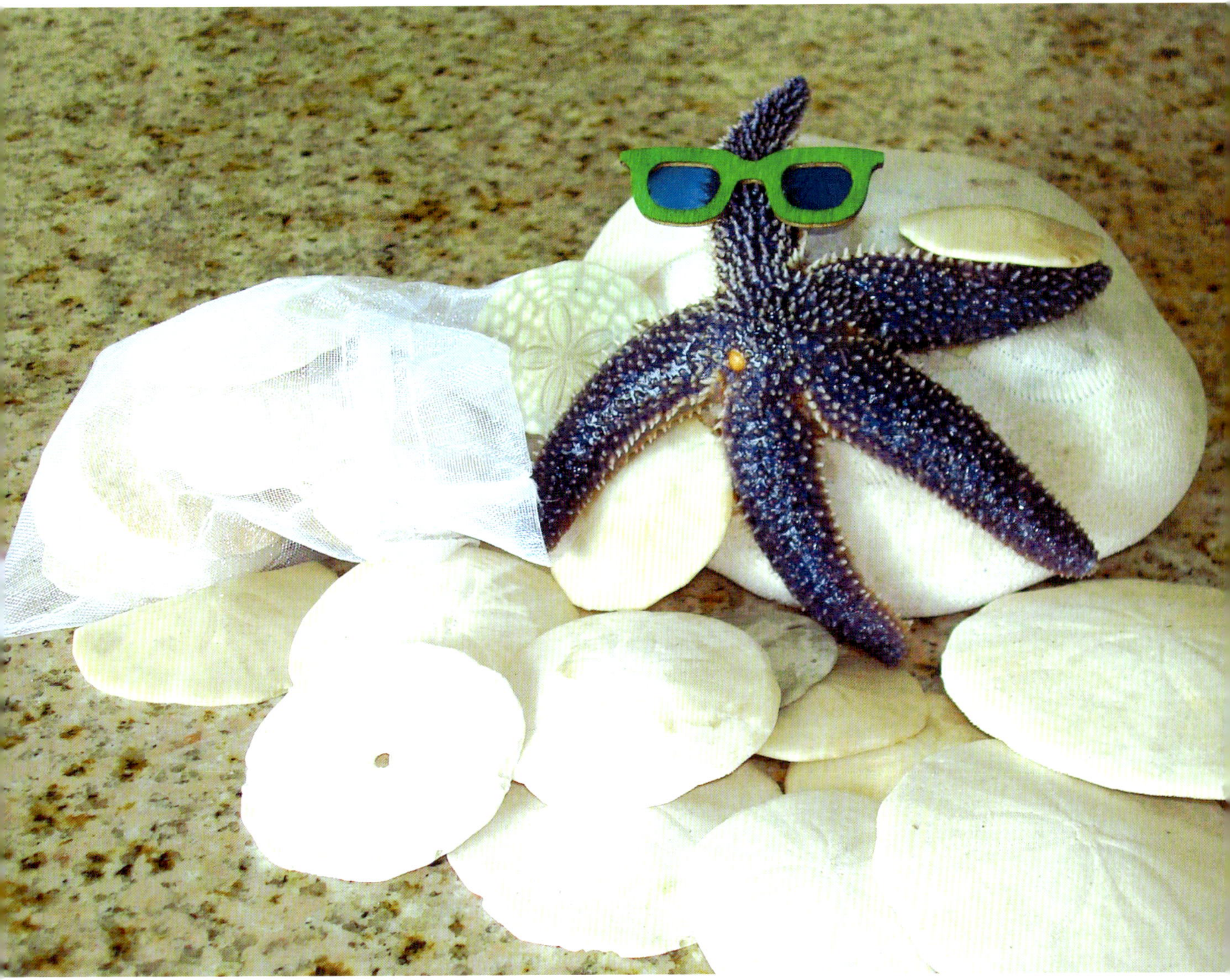

WE HAVE OUR OWN CURRENCY DOWN HERE.

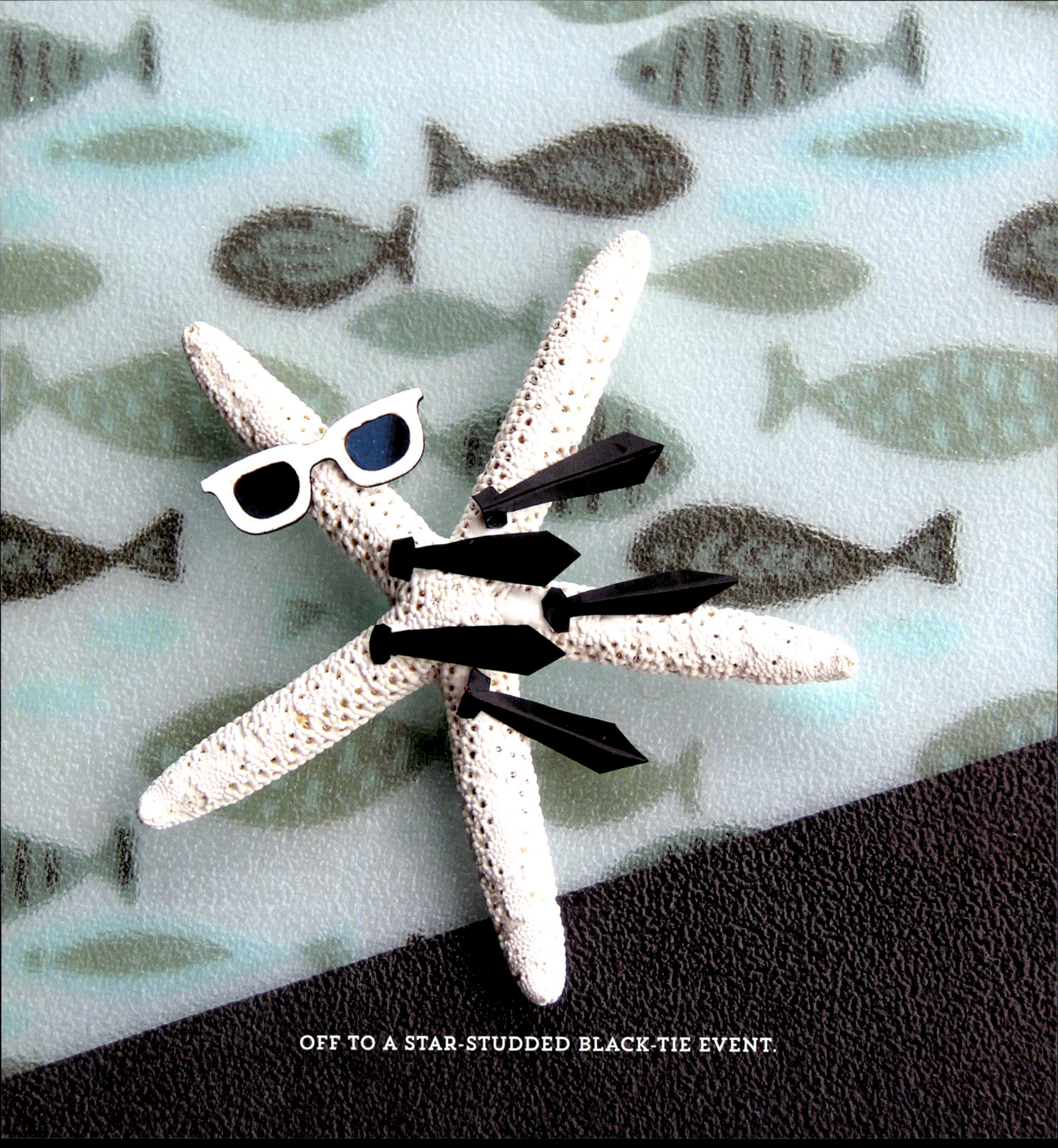

OFF TO A STAR-STUDDED BLACK-TIE EVENT.

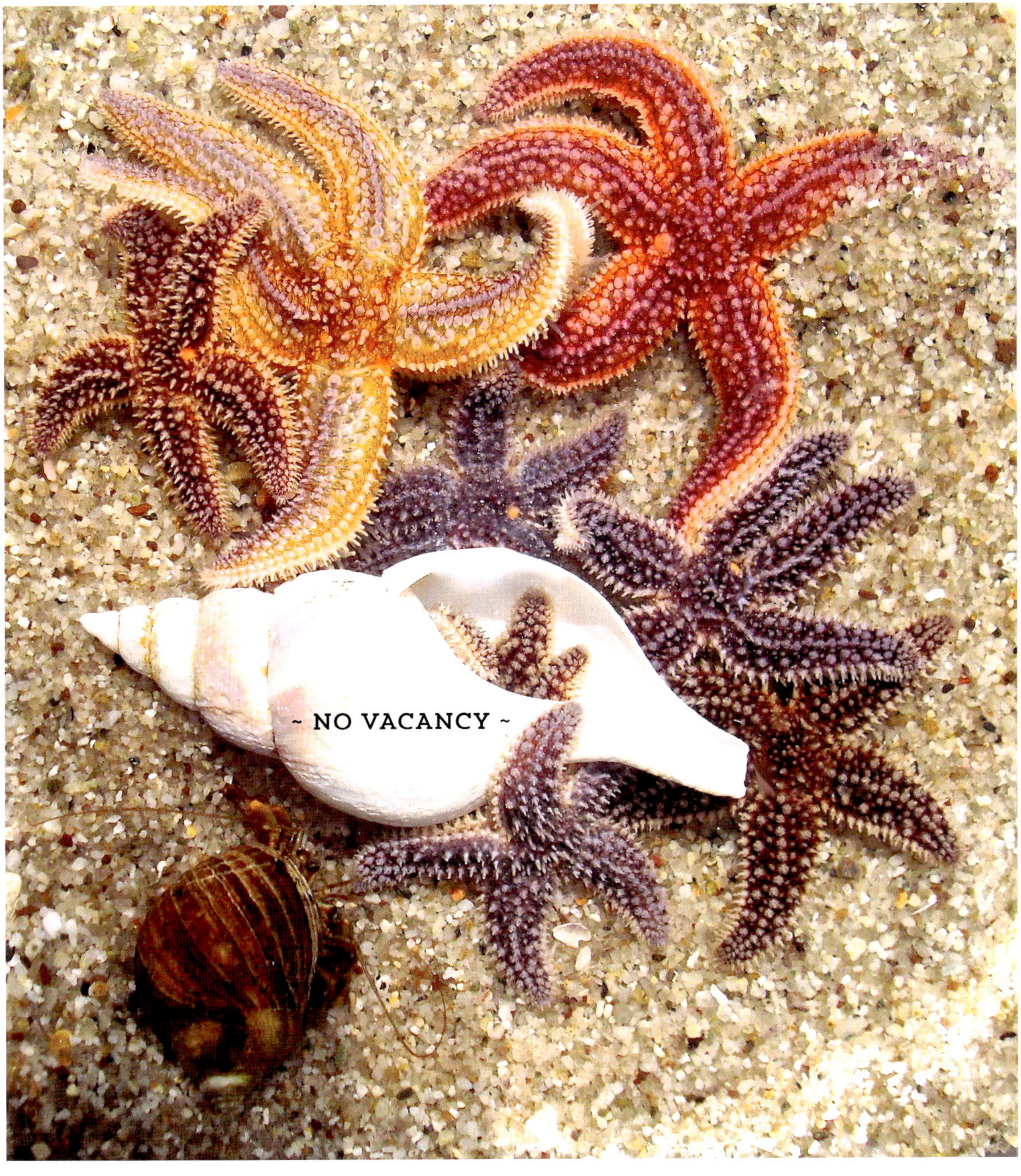
~ NO VACANCY ~

I'M FLATTERED TO BE CALLED A
COOKIE-CUTTER STARFISH.

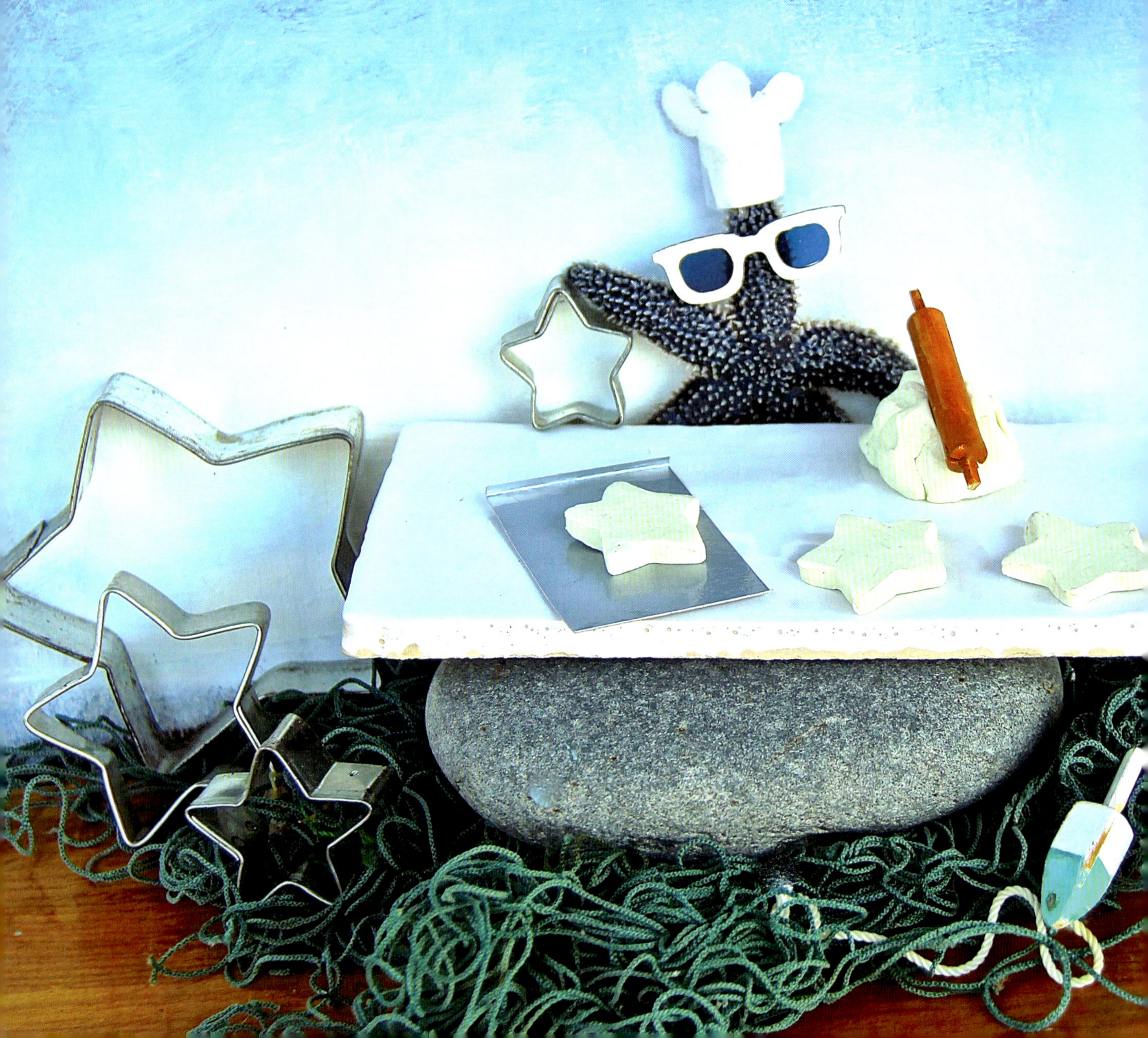

STARS, TOO, MAKE WISHES!

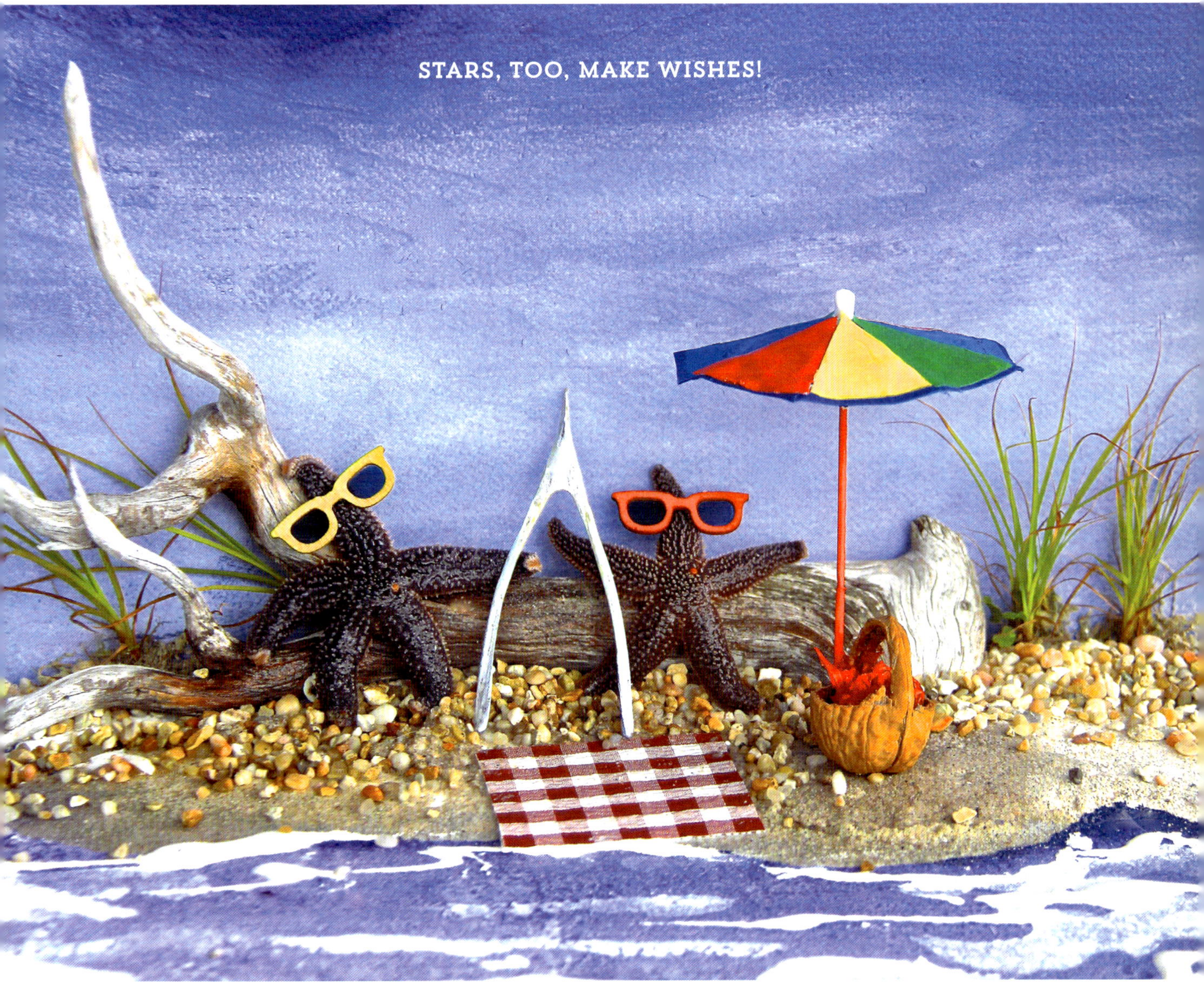

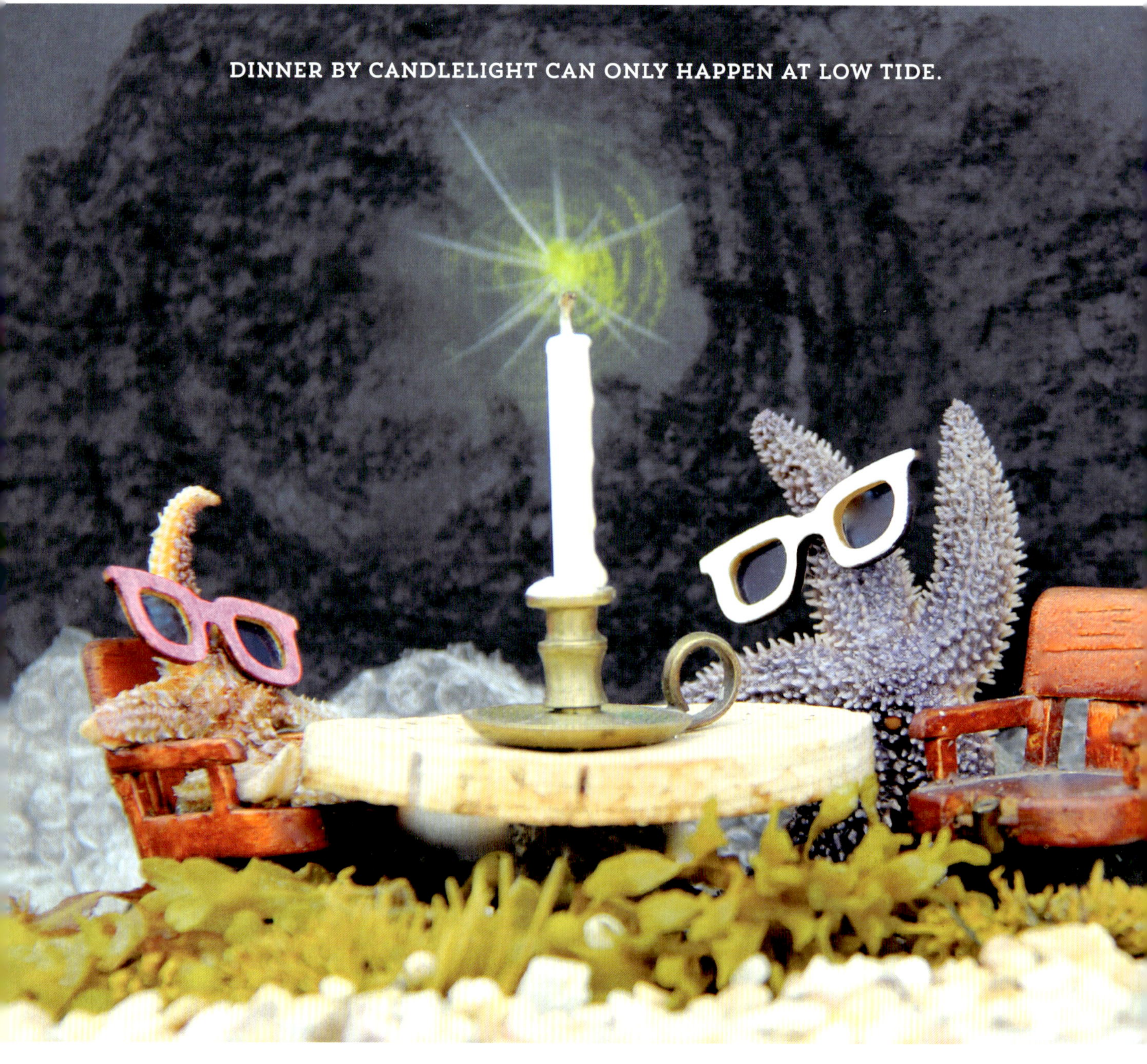
DINNER BY CANDLELIGHT CAN ONLY HAPPEN AT LOW TIDE.

DRESSING FOR WINTER IS COMPLICATED
WHEN YOU HAVE FIVE ARMS.

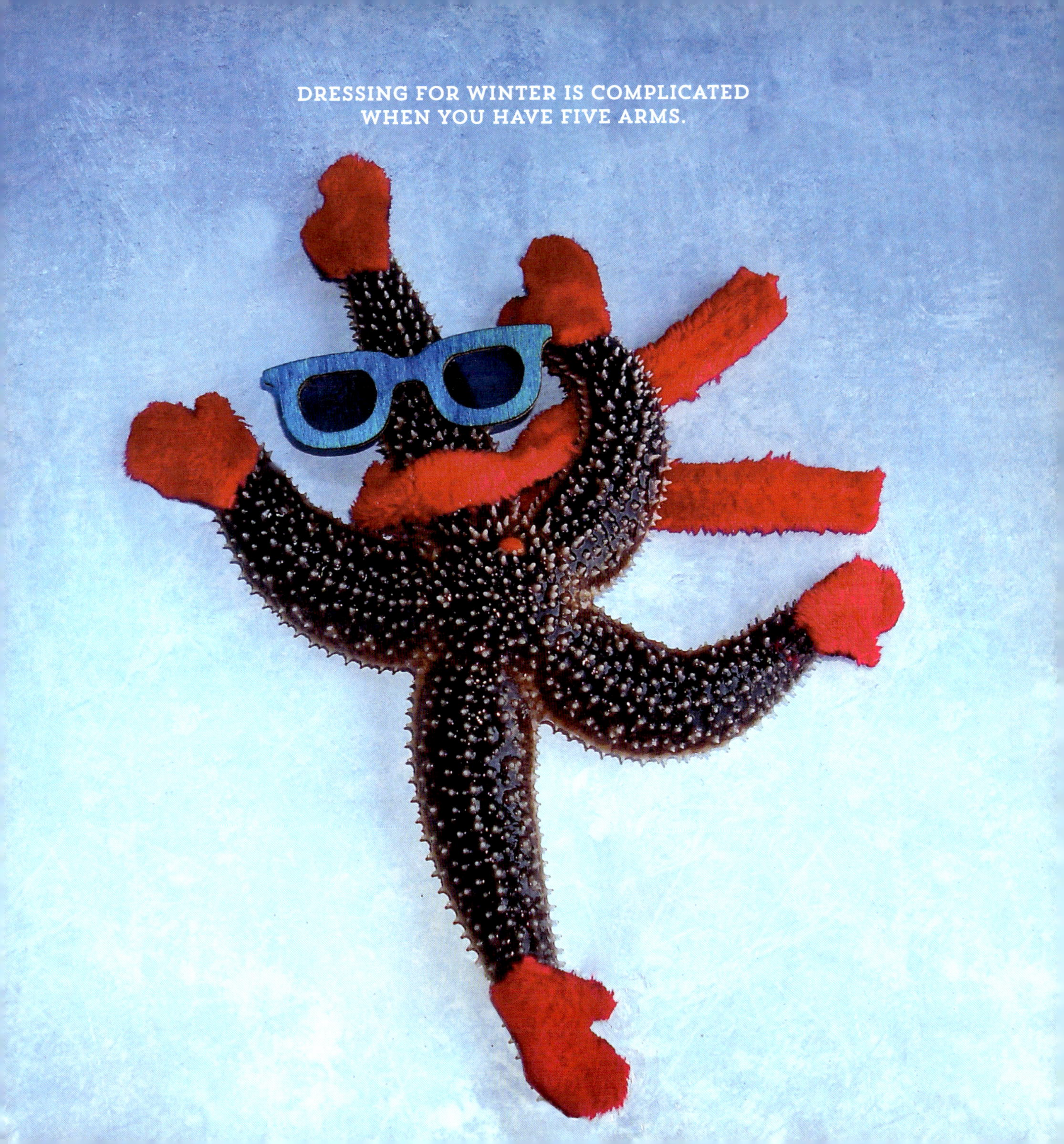

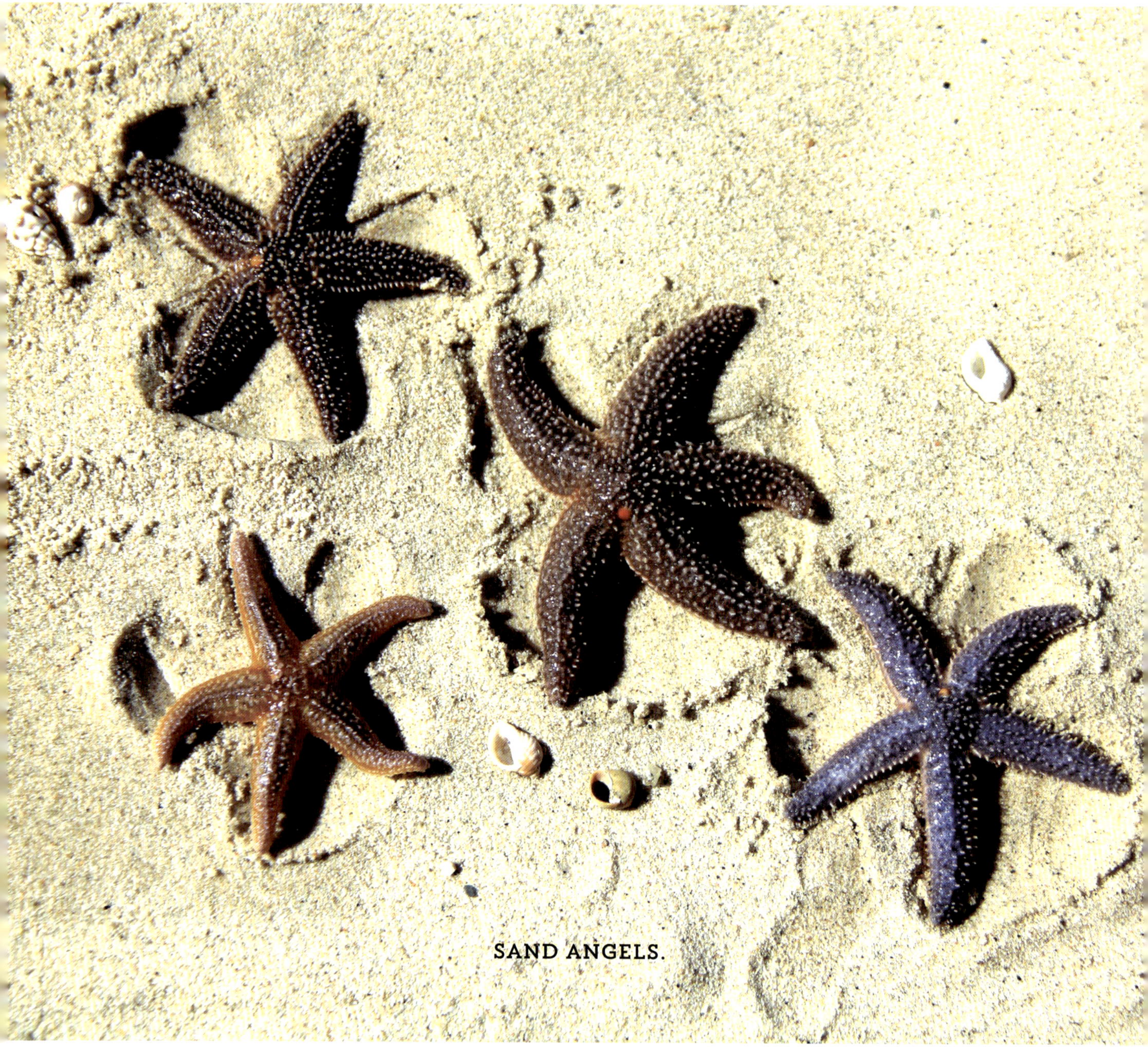

SAND ANGELS.

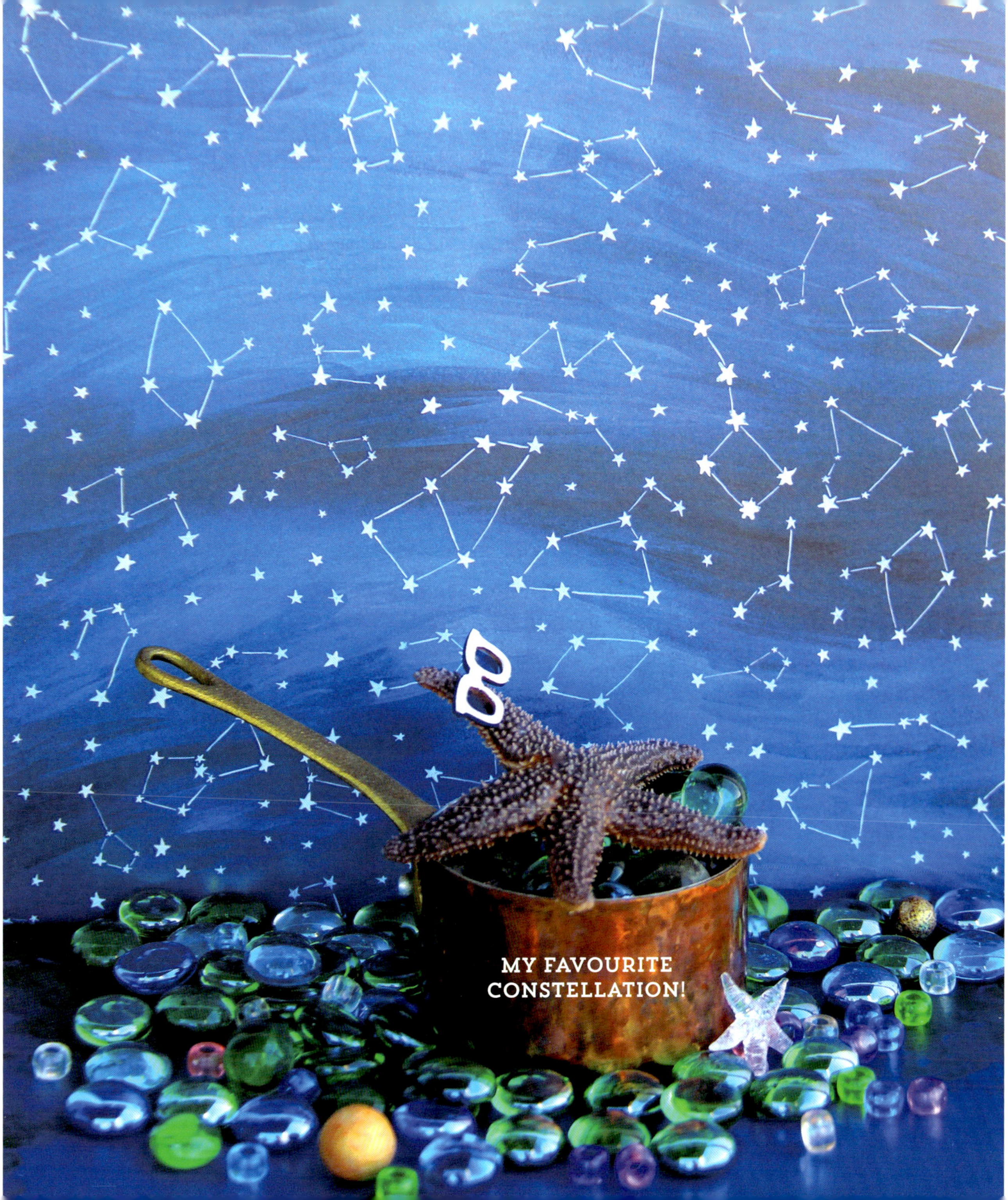
MY FAVOURITE
CONSTELLATION!

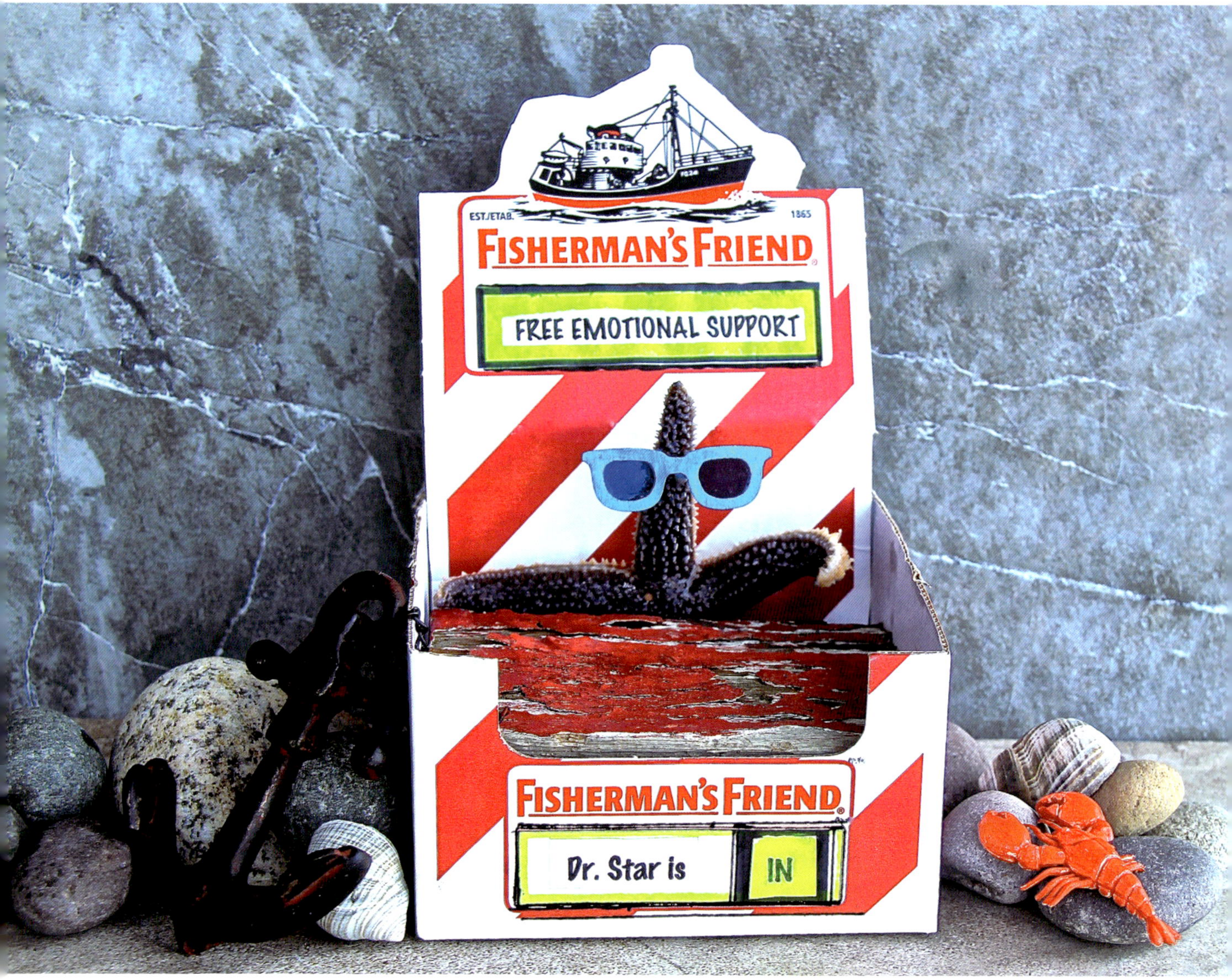

MAKING A LIVING AT SEA CAN BE TOUGH.

MANY-ARMS WRESTLING MATCH.

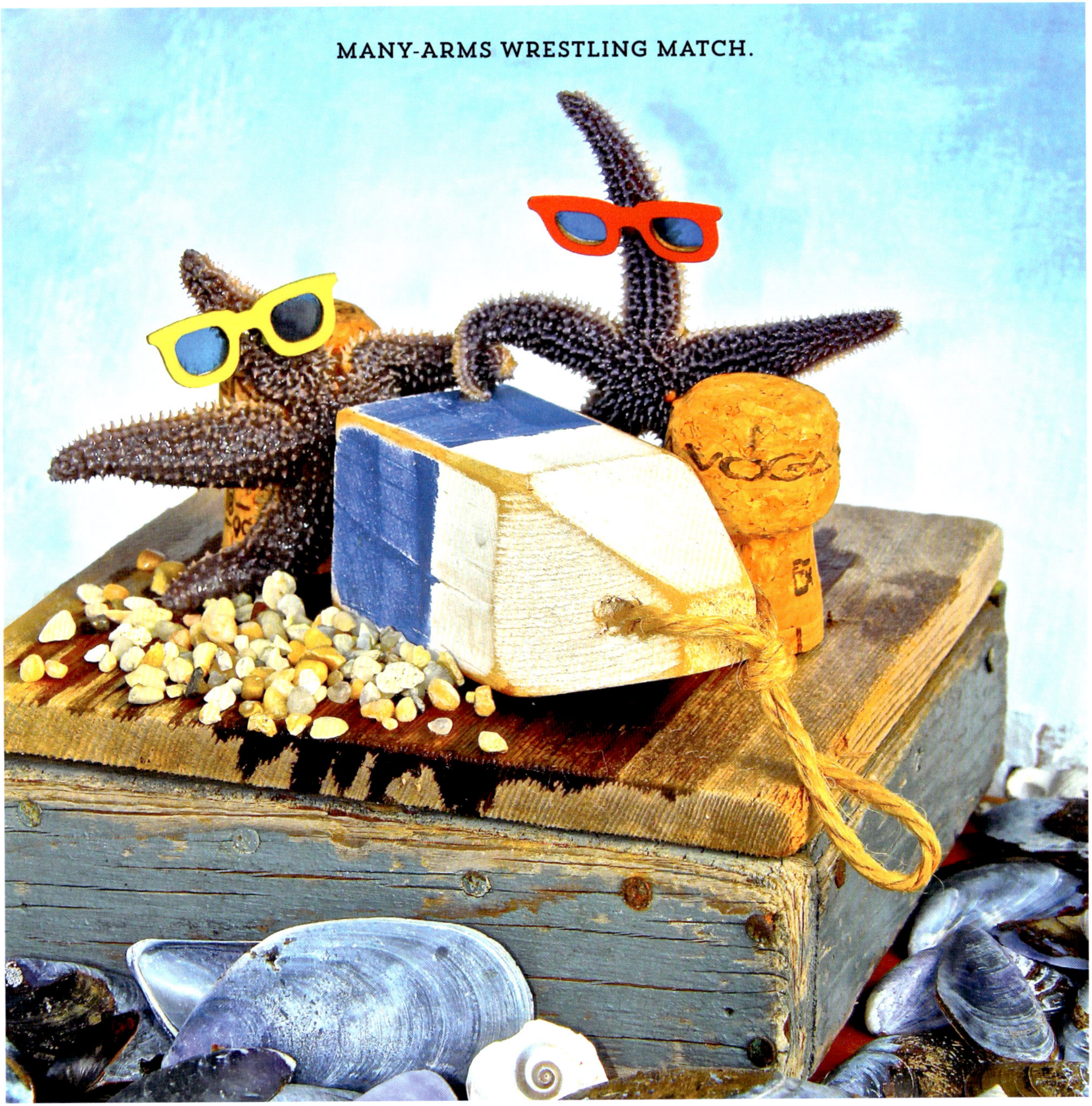

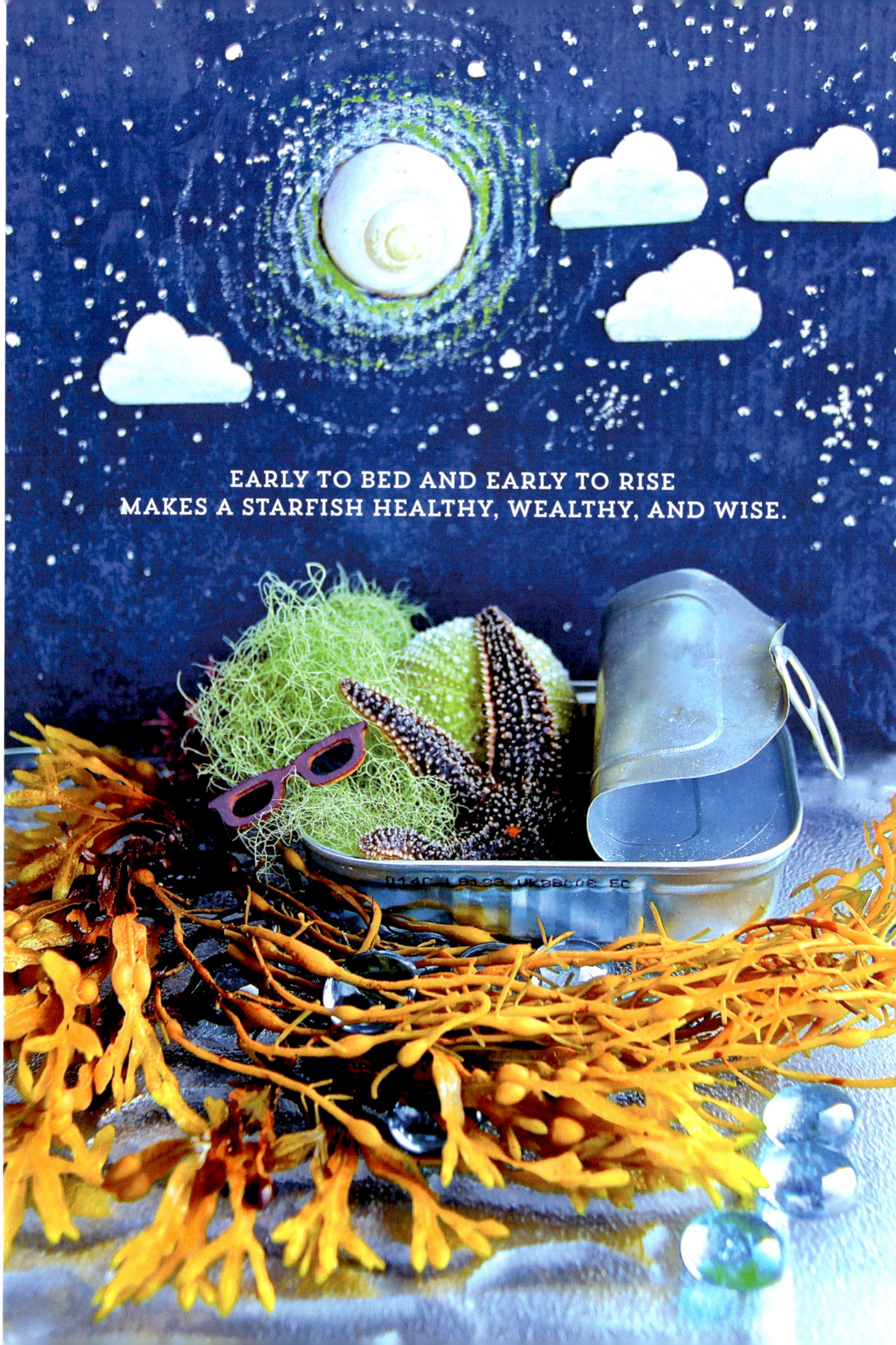

EARLY TO BED AND EARLY TO RISE
MAKES A STARFISH HEALTHY, WEALTHY, AND WISE.

A VACATION MUST INCLUDE SANDY TOES AND SALTY KISSES.

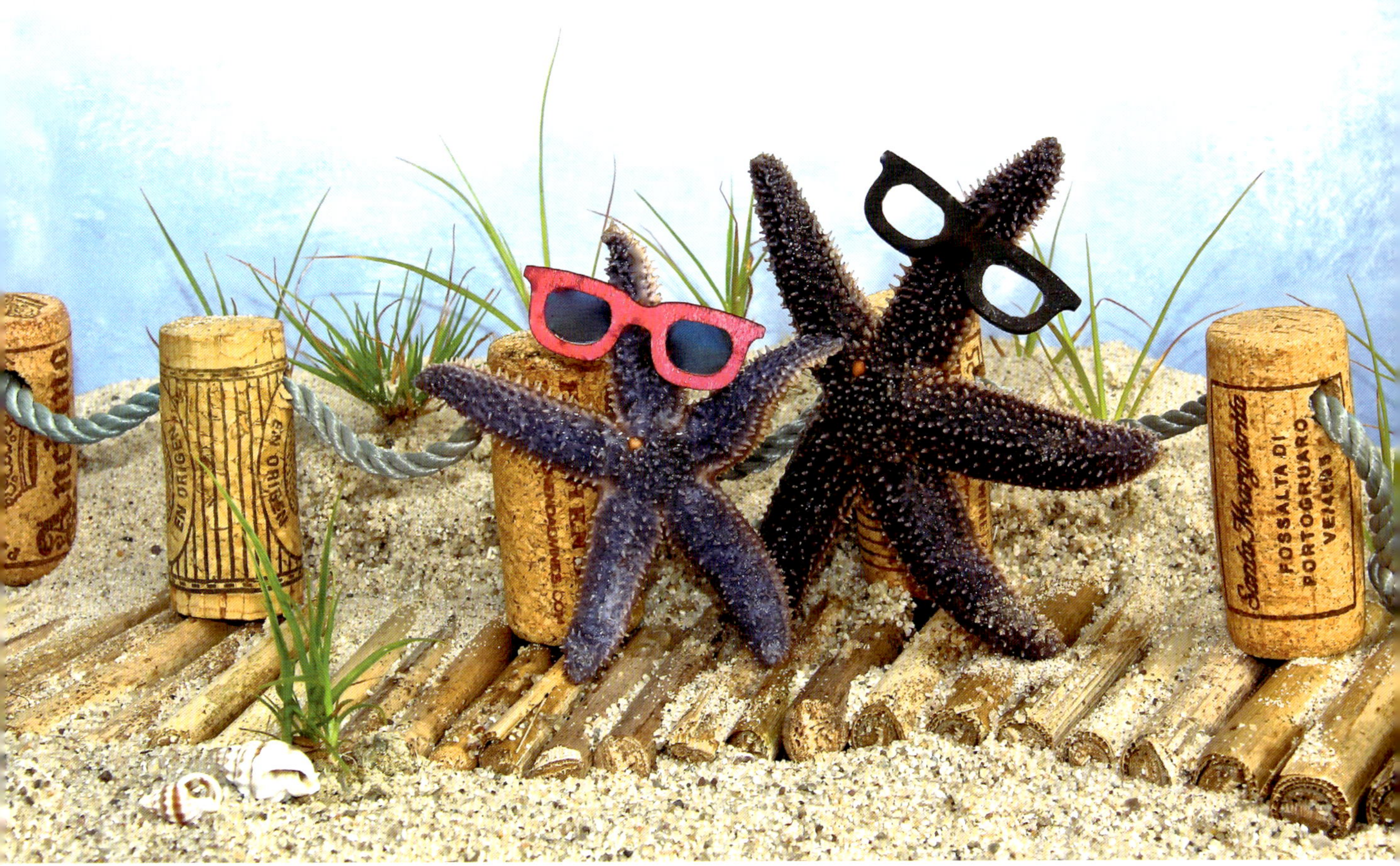

STAR OF THE CLASS.

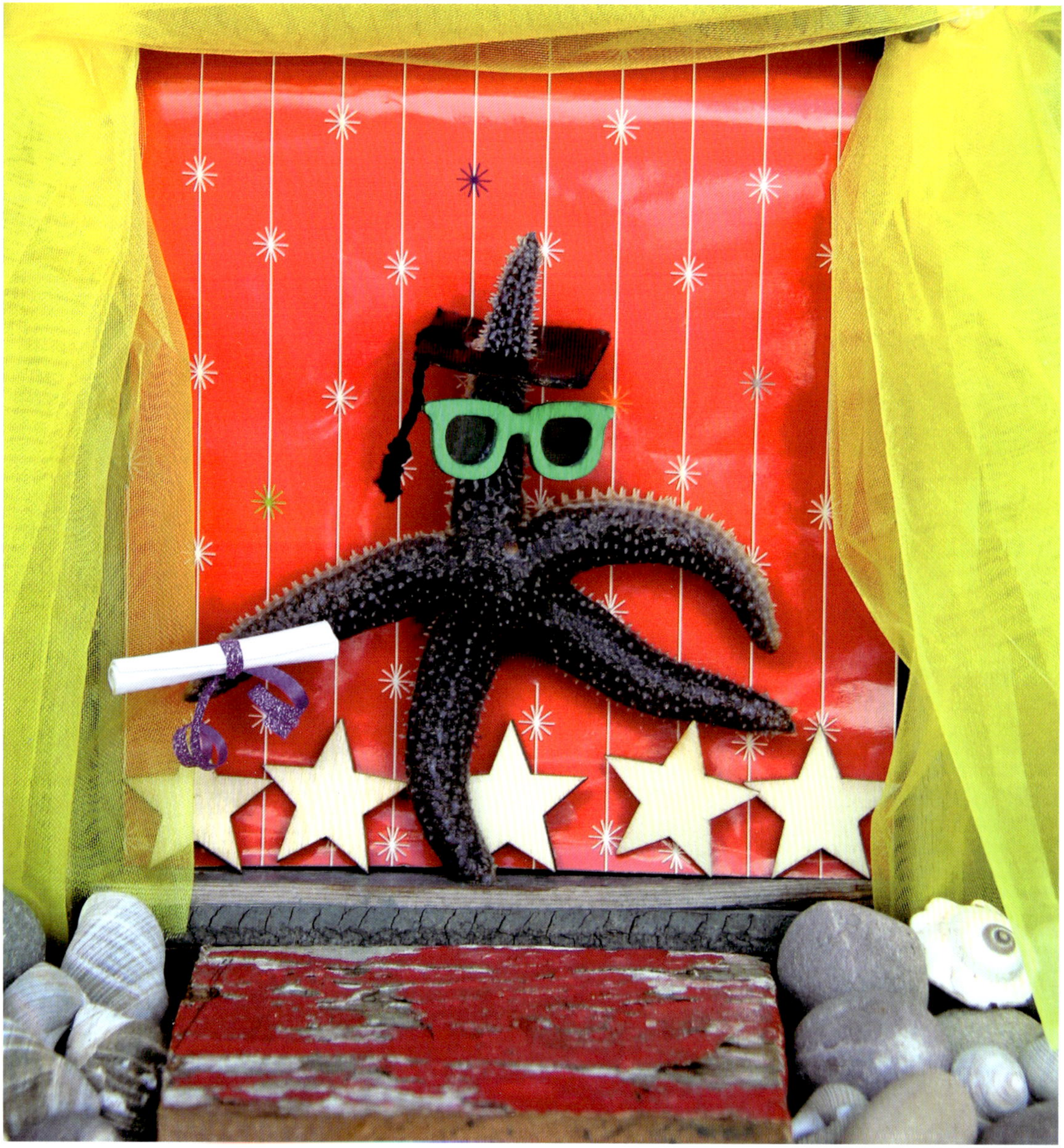

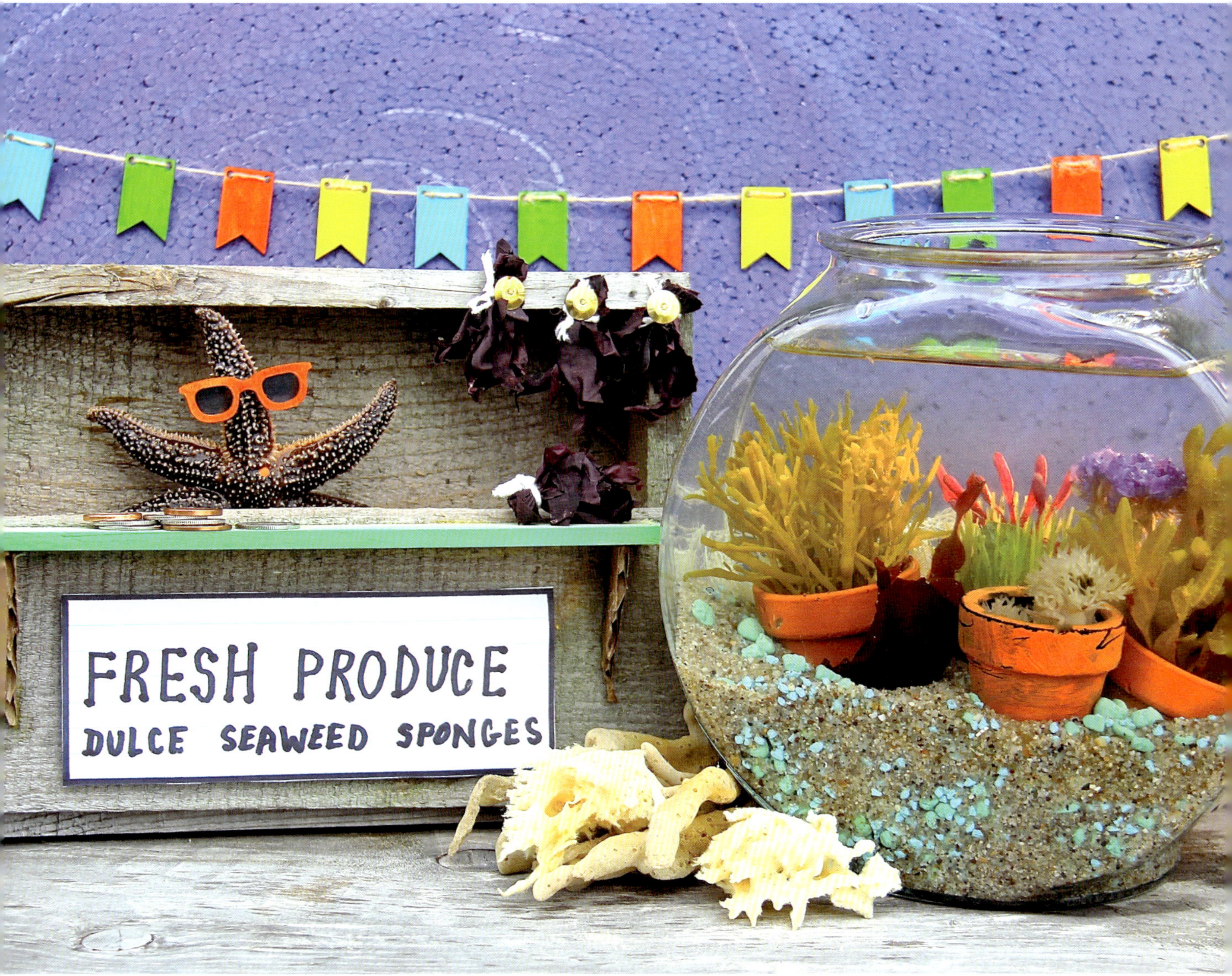

AQUATIC FARMERS' MARKET.

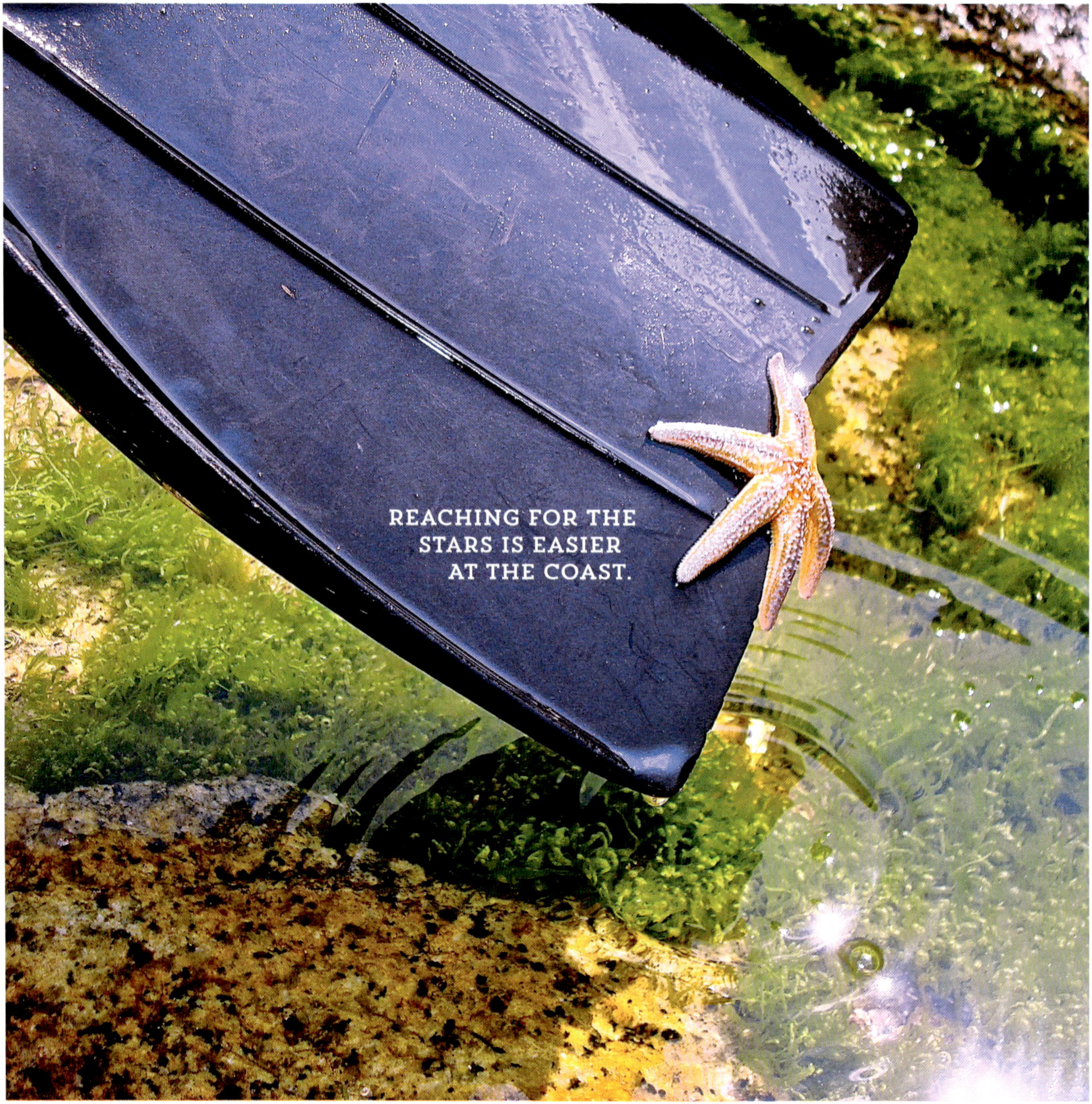
REACHING FOR THE
STARS IS EASIER
AT THE COAST.

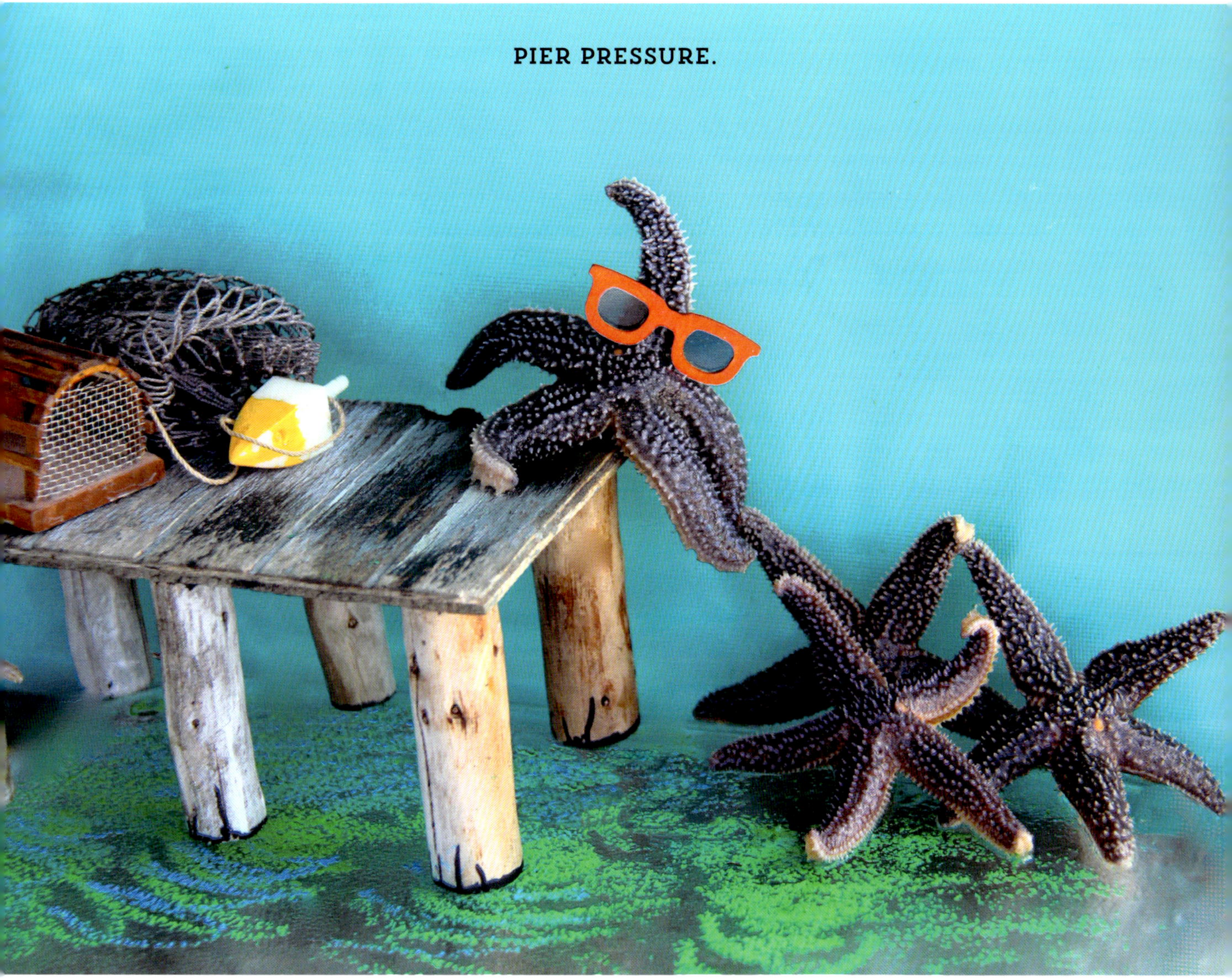
PIER PRESSURE.

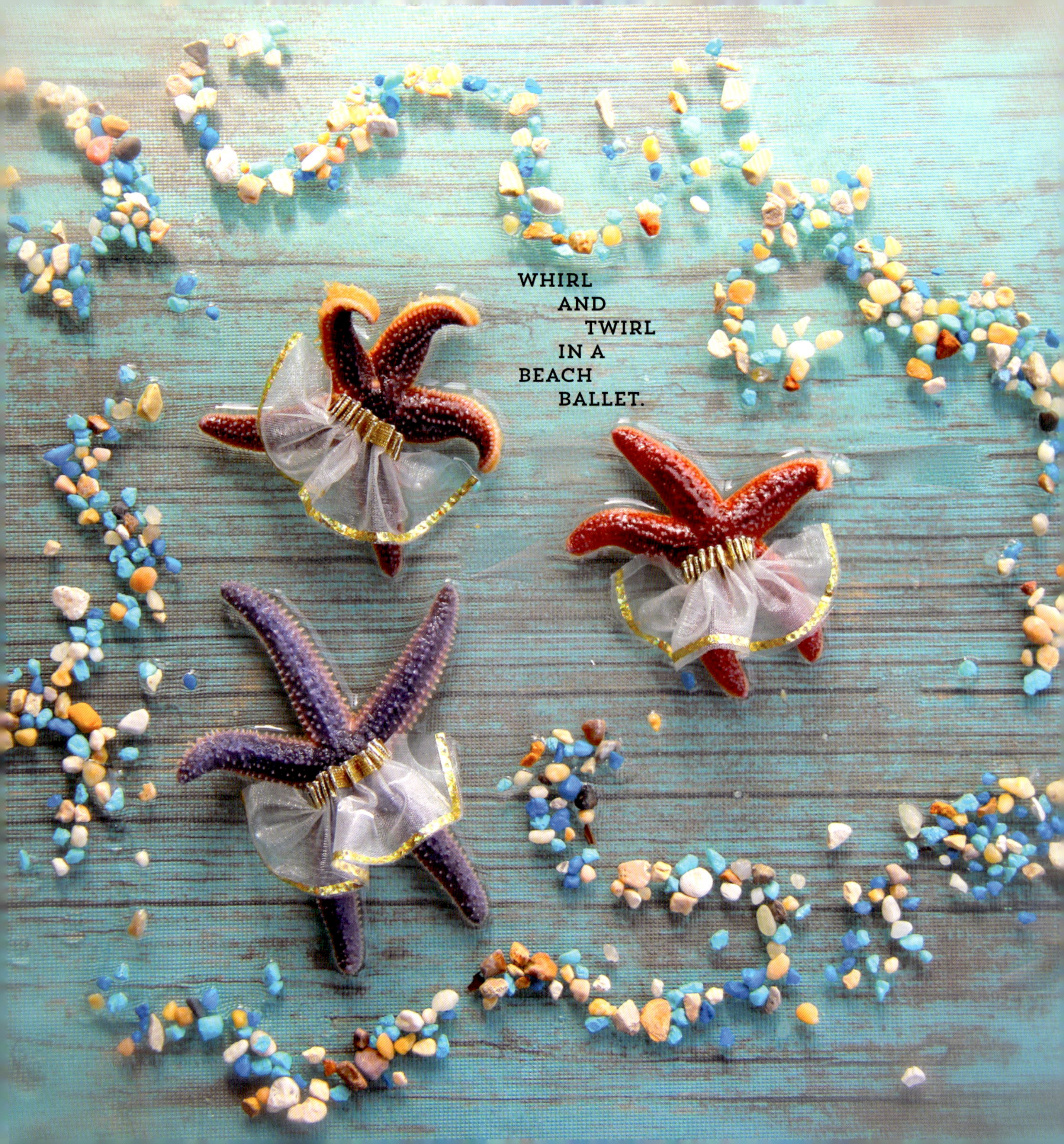

WHIRL
AND
TWIRL
IN A
BEACH
BALLET.

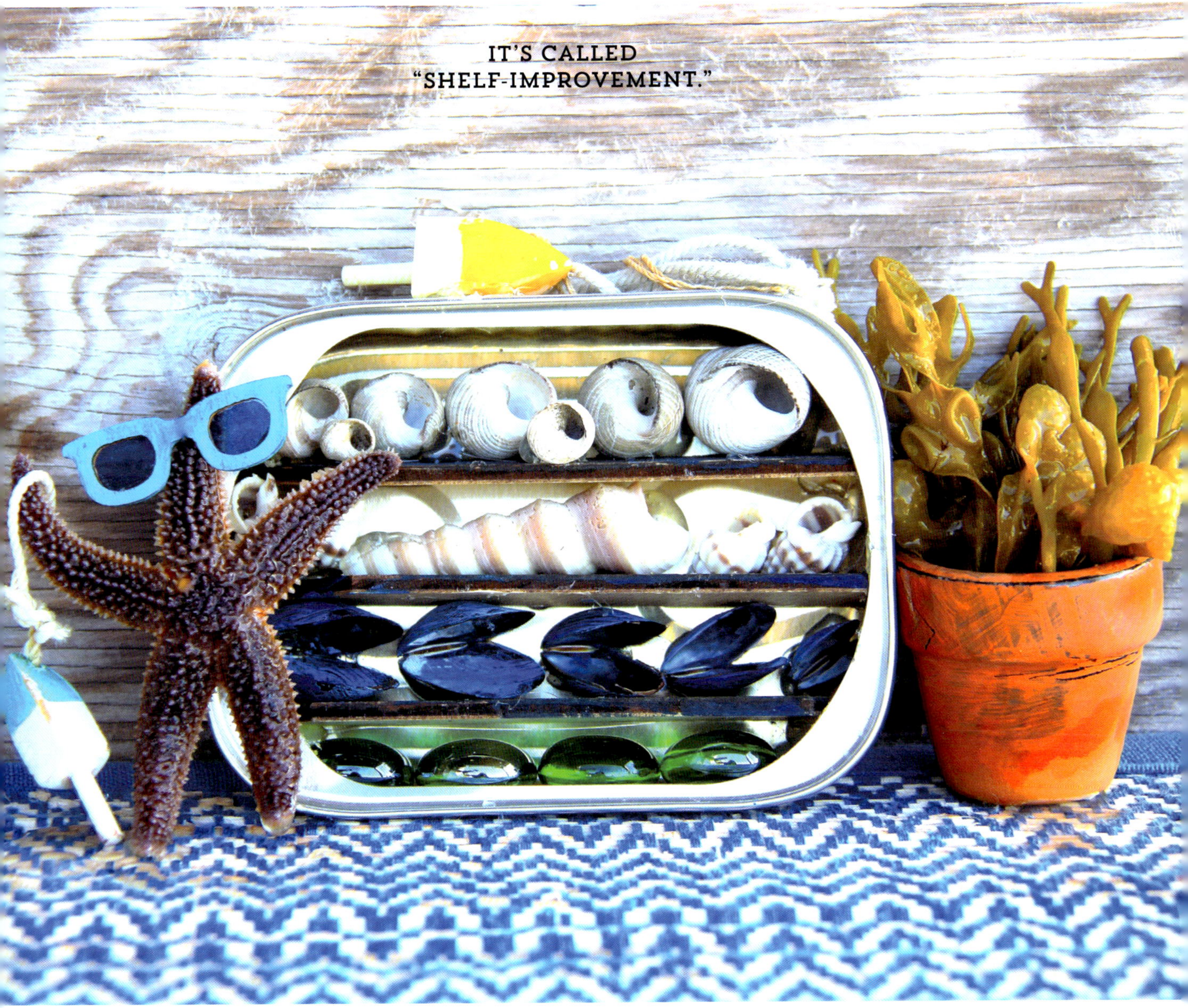
IT'S CALLED
"SHELF-IMPROVEMENT."

AND REMEMBER: NATURAL AREAS BELONG TO THE STARS OF THE COAST.

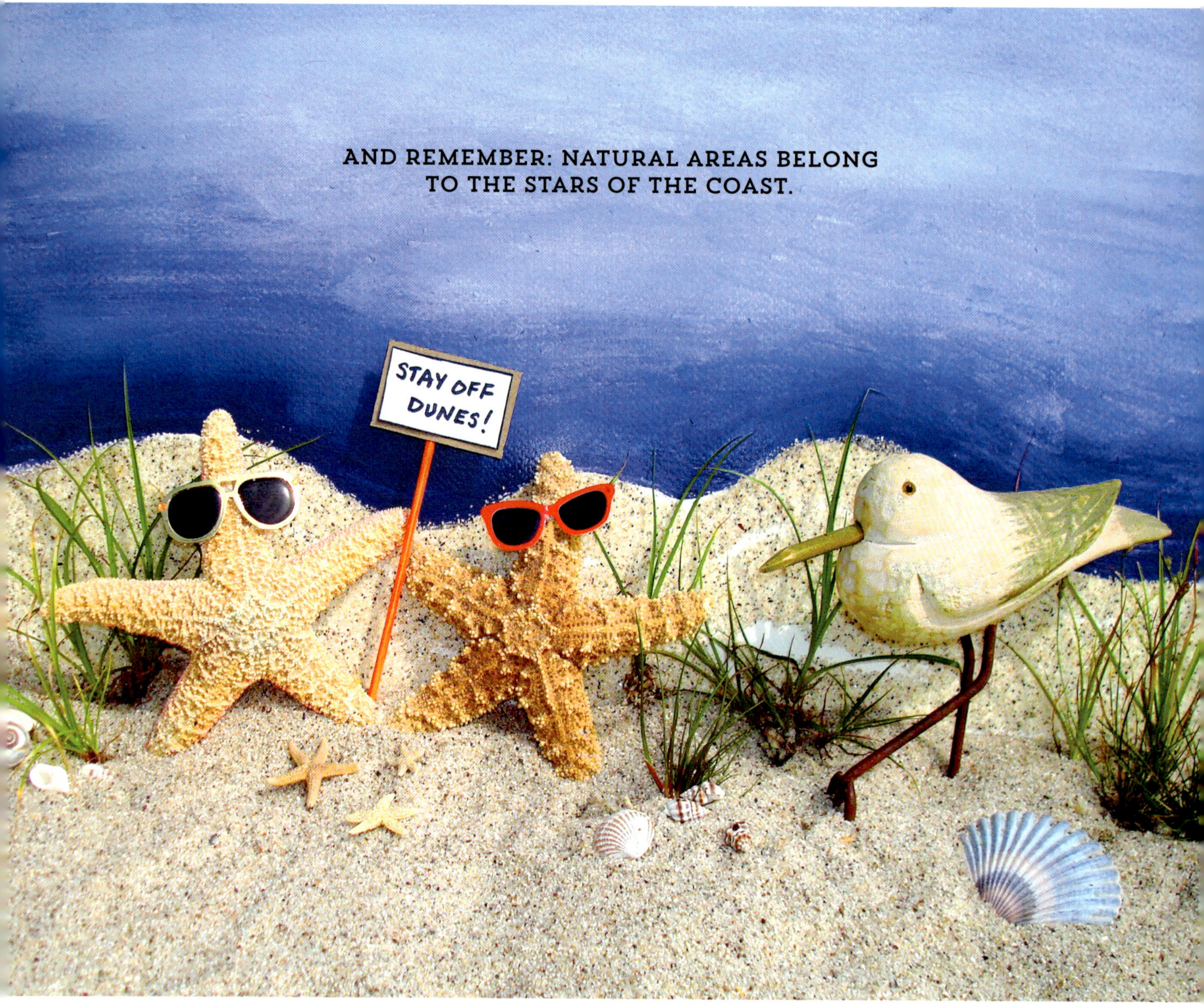

Fun Starfish Facts

- Starfish are not fish at all! They are actually related to sand dollars and sea urchins.
- Starfish live in all the oceans of the world and can be found at any depth at any water temperature.
- There are no freshwater starfish. They die when exposed to water without salt.
- Starfish have at least five arms, but some species have as many as forty!
- Each arm has an eyespot at the tip that detects light and dark.
- Starfish can regrow lost arms.
- They have no head, no brain, no mouth, no bones, no heart, and no blood. Instead they have a water vascular system to distribute nutrients to all the organs.
- Starfish eat by extending a tiny stomach out from their underside. It wraps around the meal and re-enters the body once the food source is digested.
- Starfish travel using thousands of minuscule wiggly "legs" called cilia on the underside of each arm.

A Note About Starfish Care

Starfish belong in the sea, but now and then, particularly after a storm, I find them beached, along with driftwood, seaweed, and other jetsam and flotsam. They can survive out of water for several hours until the next tide comes in—as long as they stay cool and damp. The starfish that end up above the high-water mark, however, quickly succumb to dehydration. I did make use of a few well-preserved sea stars in some photo shoots.

The great majority of my photo shoots, however, were done using robust live starfish that I collected directly from the sea in tidal pools or during shallow dives at low tide. I live along a pristine piece of coastline near Peggys Cove in St. Margaret's Bay, Nova Scotia, so access to them was quite easy. I placed the lovely creatures in a mesh bag and took them up to be kept in my refrigerator for no more than four to five days at a time. Their seawater was changed twice daily. My stars were fed servings of baby mussels that I scraped off the side of our wharf and small chopped legs of green crab (yes, that invasive one) that seagulls leave behind after a meal. I kept a bag of food in the freezer for those days when I couldn't gather it fresh. If a star did not appear to eat (a sign of distress), I took it back to the sea.

I kept as many as a dozen stars at a time because I did not want to disturb stars that were feeding. You see, it's a three-to-four-hour process for them. Another reason for keeping several stars in a bin is that certain photo shoots required an "expressive" pose. I achieved this by placing objects of various shapes in their temporary environment and waited to see which star would twist to suit the shoot best. The scene sets were prepared in advance, and my camera was in position and ready to click as soon as the *stars of the show* were in place. I was always careful not to keep the stars out of water for any more than five minutes. All photos were taken outside in natural light—no hot lamps.

I can thank about sixty individual live starfish for lending me their wondrous grace and beauty for this book. Each was returned safely to the sea, perhaps a little chubbier than when I found them.

If you ever come across live beached starfish, show them true love by returning them to the safety of the body of water from which they came.